THE AZTEC·NEWS

Author: PHILIP STEELE ◆ Consultants: PENNY BATEMAN & NORMA ROSSO

Dear Reader,

Almost 200 years have passed since our great city of Tenochtitlán was founded, and here at THE AZTEC NEWS we think it's the perfect time to celebrate the many achievements of our nation.

So we've hunted back through past copies of our newspaper to find the stories that really made the headlines and rewritten them for this special edition. We've included feature articles, too, on all aspects of our everyday life — from feasts and farming to gods and gambling!

We are proud to present this celebratory edition of THE AZTEC NEWS, and we hope that you will treasure it always.

The Editor in Chief

Philip Steele

A NOTE FROM OUR PUBLISHER

As we all know, the Aztecs didn't really have newspapers. But if they had, we're sure they would all have been reading *The Aztec News*!
We hope you enjoy it.

Candlewick Press

CANDLEWICK PRESS
CAMBRIDGE, MASSACHUSETTS

CONTENTS

MAP OF THE AZTEC EMPIRE

HUAXTEC PEOPLE

CHICHIMEC PEOPLE

THE VALLEY OF MEXICO

Tlacopan

Texcoco

Tenochtitlán

TLAXCALAN PEOPLE

Gulf of Mexico

Veracruz

TEOTITLÁN PEOPLE

Coixtlahuaca

YOPITZINGO PEOPLE

MIXTEC PEOPLE

Pacific Ocean

MAYAN PEOPLE

NORTH AMERICA

SOUTH AMERICA

THE VALLEY OF MEXICO

Lake Zumpango

Lake Xaltocan

Lake Texcoco

Tenochtitlán

Lake Chalco

Lake Xochimilco

N
W   E
S

Extent of the Aztec Empire at A.D. 1521

HOME AT LAST

Illustrated by CHRIS FORSEY

FINAL RESTING PLACE: Once a barren island, Tenochtitlán is now home to more than 250,000 people.

NEARLY 400 YEARS have passed since our ancestors set out to find a new home for our people. In memory of their courage, *The Aztec News* recounts the story of the long and dangerous journey that led to the founding of our great city.

ACCORDING to the tales retold by generations of storytellers, this journey began in about A.D. 1100.

In those days, our people were living far to the northwest of where our home is today.

Then Huitzilopochtli, the main god of our tribe, told them to leave their homes and travel south.

For almost 100 years our ancestors roamed the land, climbing mountain passes and crossing vast deserts. Life was hard — while they were on the move, our people were forced to eat whatever wild animals and plants they could find.

Many times they tried to settle and grow crops, but always Huitzilopochtli ordered them to move on.

At last, in about the year 1200, our ancestors came to the green and fertile Valley of Mexico.

But everywhere they turned, they found other tribes had already settled on the best land and built cities. There seemed to be nowhere left for our people to go.

SETTLED IN A SWAMP

Our ancestors begged for help and were given an area of snake-infested swampland that no one else wanted. And for over 100 years they worked for the other tribes and struggled to survive on the land they had been given.

Our ancestors thought that Huitzilopochtli had forgotten his people. But then he spoke to them one more time.

He told them to move on and they would see an eagle settle on a cactus growing from a

EAGLE ON A CACTUS: The symbol of our city.

rock. This would be a sign, showing them this was the place to make their home.

Of course, we all know how the story ends. Our priests did see an eagle land on a cactus. The cactus was on an island in Lake Texcoco. And this was where, in 1325, our ancestors came to rest.

They planted crops and built houses and temples. And in time, our great city of Tenochtitlán rose from the sparkling waters of the lake.

The years in the wilderness were over. At long last we had found our home.

29 GLORIOUS YEARS

Illustrated by CHRIS MOLAN

IN 1469, OUR PEOPLE mourned the death of Montezuma I, the great man who won a mighty empire for our nation. *The Aztec News* looks back at the life of one of our most powerful rulers.

WHEN Montezuma came to the throne in 1440, he was already known as a skilled warrior. But there was more to Montezuma than simply bravery in battle. He soon showed himself to be a wise and ambitious ruler.

With the help of the neighboring cities of Tlacopan and Texcoco, we had already gained control of many of the other peoples living in the Valley of Mexico.

Montezuma was quick to claim his share of the tribute payments due to him from these conquered peoples — gifts of precious stones and metals, as well as food and clothing. Any who refused were swiftly punished by our warriors.

FLOODS SWAMP FUTURE PLANS

Montezuma wanted to conquer other tribes, but his plans were delayed when Tenochtitlán was destroyed by floods in 1452. Two hard years of famine followed.

Montezuma was not to be defeated, though. He had a large dam built to protect the city from future floods. A system of aqueducts was also constructed to channel fresh water across from the mainland.

Then in 1458, when our city was strong once more, Montezuma sent our armies out to make new conquests.

City after city fell before the might of our warriors. Vast numbers of captives were taken in battle and brought back to Tenochtitlán to be sacrificed to our gods.

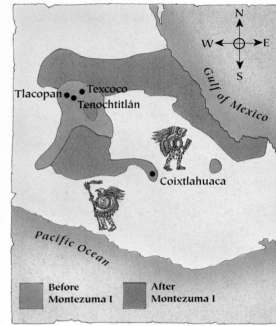

BEFORE AND AFTER: Land won by Montezuma I.

And in return, the gods rewarded us with even greater victories.

Within just ten years, Montezuma was ruling over millions of people living in hundreds of cities across the land. And he controlled the whole of this vast empire from our glorious city of Tenochtitlán.

Montezuma's power was so great, and our warriors were so feared, that we did not need to put in rulers of our own to govern these conquered peoples.

Nor did we force them to change their beliefs.

As is our custom, we simply made them agree to honor our gods in addition to their own.

And we sent a tribute collector to each of the tribes we defeated to make certain that regular tribute payments were made to Montezuma.

Each year, thousands of tons of food and cotton clothing flooded into Tenochtitlán, along with luxury goods, such as precious green quetzal feathers, black obsidian glass, turquoise stone, and gold craftwork.

And with this vast wealth, Montezuma made us the richest and most envied of all the tribes living between the two seas.

AWESOME ARRAY: Montezuma I is presented with tribute goods by conquered tribes.

SUCCESS IS OURS!

Illustrated by ANGUS McBRIDE

OUR VICTORY over the Mixtec city of Coixtlahuaca in 1458 marked the start of our triumphant rise to power under Montezuma I. A reporter from *The Aztec News* witnessed the final battle and sent back this report.

CLASH OF STRENGTH: The Mixtecs are forced back by our Jaguar and Eagle warriors.

I AM STANDING in the center of Coixtlahuaca. All around me, the streets are filled with dead and dying Mixtecs.

The sky is thick with smoke as the Mixtec temple goes up in flames. This fire is a triumphant sign to the world that victory is ours.

Ahead of me, I can see our army's finest warriors, the Eagles and the Jaguars, rounding up captives to be sent back to our city for sacrifice.

Today's events bring to a close one of the largest campaigns we Aztecs have ever waged. There were more than 200,000 warriors in the army that left Tenochtitlán, along with 100,000 porters to carry their supplies.

I am told that the Mixtecs shook with fear as they saw row after row of our warriors marching toward them. No matter how hard the Mixtecs fought, they had no hope of defeating us.

This glorious victory will be remembered for years to come. Not only will the sacrifice of so many captives delight our gods, but the people of Coixtlahuaca must now pay a high price if they wish to be left in peace.

The Mixtecs are known throughout the land for the wealth of their traders and the fine skills of their craftworkers. The tribute payments they must send to Montezuma will fill his treasury with riches.

And this is just the beginning. May the gods bless Montezuma with many more victories!

MIXTEC PEACE PAYMENT

IT'S A RECORD! A scribe's list of Mixtec tribute.

Since their defeat, the people of Coixtlahuaca have had to send regular payments of tribute to Tenochtitlán.

As with all such tribute payments, each item has been recorded by scribes.

The examples you see here show just a little of the immense wealth that the Mixtec conquest has brought us.

❖ **Wooden shields** decorated with priceless feathers

❖ **Necklaces of carved greenstone**

❖ **Bags of dried cochineal beetles** for making red dye

❖ **Bundles of quetzal feathers**

❖ **Finely woven blankets**

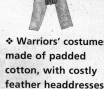
❖ **Warriors' costumes** made of padded cotton, with costly feather headdresses

Illustrated by VANESSA CARD

EMPIRE AT RISK

Illustrated by CHRISTIAN HOOK

MONTEZUMA I's empire almost fell apart in the years that followed his rule. Then, in 1486, Ahuizotl came to the throne...

FOR NEARLY 20 years after Montezuma's death in 1469, our nation was without a powerful ruler. Our warriors had lost heart, and our army was no longer feared.

Things had become so bad that some cities in the Huaxtec region were even refusing to make tribute payments.

But when Ahuizotl came to the throne, he immediately set about proving to the world that a strong man was back in charge.

ON THE WARPATH

Ahuizotl's first move was to restore the fearsome reputation of our army by teaching the Huaxtec rebels a lesson they would never forget.

He encouraged his men by marching into battle beside them. And he fought with such skill and ferocity that they were inspired to match his courage.

Our army stormed city after city, burning Huaxtec temples and sending back thousands of captives for sacrifice in Tenochtitlán.

With the Huaxtecs under control, Ahuizotl went on to conquer new territories — until our empire stretched from coast to coast.

And once again, we were the mightiest and most feared nation in all the land. 🔲

ALL POWERFUL:
Ahuizotl in his ceremonial finery.

WHAT

IN 1487, THE MOST awesome and impressive ceremony our nation has ever seen was held in honor of the reopening of our Great Temple. A reporter from *The Aztec News* was at the scene.

AS THE SUN rose over the city this morning, I watched in awe while our glorious ruler, Ahuizotl, slowly climbed the steps of the Great Temple.

Around me, crowds of people stood in silence as we waited for our ruler to reach the twin shrines at the top of the steps. We knew that once there, the priests would hand him a sacrificial knife and the ceremony would begin.

The first two captives slowly climbed the twin stairways of the temple. When they reached the top, the priests took hold of them and laid them on the stone altars.

Ahuizotl approached and swiftly cut out each captive's heart. Then the next two captives were placed on the altars.

When Ahuizotl was exhausted, he invited the rulers of our loyal allies, the cities of Tlacopan and Texcoco, to take his place. And when they became tired, our priests carried on.

DOUBLE CELEBRATION

This grand occasion is being held to mark the completion of the sixth rebuilding of the Great Temple. But it is also a magnificent celebration of our glorious ruler's recent victory against the Huaxtec rebels.

There are said to be tens of thousands of captives — so many, in fact, that the sacrifices are expected to take at least four days.

A SPECTACLE!

Illustrated by LUIGI GALANTE

FINAL FOOTSTEPS: Captives line up at the foot of the Great Temple, before climbing the steep steps to their death.

TEMPLE FACTS

The Great Temple of Tenochtitlán stands at the center of our city and is the sacred center of our world.

❁

At the very top of the temple are the twin shrines to our two most important gods, Huitzilopochtli and Tlaloc.

❁

The first temple was made from reeds and mud. It was built in 1325, and it marked the spot where our ancestors saw the eagle on the cactus, the sign that showed them where to build Tenochtitlán.

❁

Since then, the Great Temple has been enlarged seven times. Each time it was made of stone and built over and around the previous one.

❁

The sixth rebuilding was finished during Ahuizotl's reign. The opening ceremony for the seventh temple was held in 1502, when Montezuma II came to the throne; the temple is now almost 200 feet high.

On this first day the captives waited patiently in line. They knew they were about to be given the greatest honor we can grant them, and that in return they will receive a blissful life after death.

The square in front of the Great Temple was packed with onlookers — every noble in our city was present.

Among them stood rulers from every city in the empire. They had been invited by Ahuizotl to attend this spectacular festival, and not one of them had dared refuse.

I spoke to one visitor, who would not give me his name.

"I was made to come," he said. "There would have been trouble for my family and my people if I hadn't.

I've watched today's events with fear and wonder — both of the gods and of the Aztecs.

I know that when I return home I will be laden with lavish gifts of clothing and jewelry. But I have also learned something here that I will never forget.

The incredible sight of thousands of captives being sacrificed on top of that colossal temple has made me realize just how powerful and ruthless you Aztecs are. Only a fool would dare to defy you."

Today, Ahuizotl has delivered a clear and unmistakable message to the world — under his rule, we Aztecs have never been so mighty or so feared. Wage war on us at your peril! 🔥

COUNTDOWN TO CONFLICT

Illustrated by IAN THOMPSON

March 1519
Stories begin to reach Tenochtitlán from the east coast, telling of tall wooden towers floating on the sea. Reports say there are 11 of these strange ships.

April 1519
Over 600 pale-skinned foreigners leave the ships and set up camp at Veracruz. Our spies learn that the men call themselves Spaniards. This news is taken to Montezuma II. He sends splendid gifts of gold to the Spanish leader, Hernán Cortés.

August 1519
The Spaniards burn their ships—do they plan never to leave our land? Riding on the great deer they call horses, they set off toward Tenochtitlán.

September 1519
Cortés persuades our enemies, the Tlaxcalan people, to join him as he marches through their land.

November 8, 1519
Cortés reaches Lake Texcoco, where he is greeted by Montezuma. The Spaniards and the Tlaxcalans are invited to stay in one of the palaces in our city.

November 24, 1519
Cortés tries to control Tenochtitlán by taking Montezuma hostage.

May 1520
At a religious festival, the Spaniards murder a number of our nobles. Fighting breaks out and the foreigners retreat to their palace.

June 1520
Montezuma tells us we must make peace with the Spaniards. These are not the words of a brave ruler.
Our nobles turn their backs on Montezuma and choose Cuitlahuac, his brother, as ruler.
Montezuma begs us to make peace, but we will listen to this traitor no longer. Instead, we pelt him with stones. He falls, the Spaniards carry him back into their palace, and he is never seen alive again.

SPANIARDS FLEE CITY

Illustrated by GINO D'ACHILLE

THIS GLORIOUS DAY, June 30, 1520, is one that our people will remember forever. At long last the Spanish cowards have been chased from our city — Tenochtitlán is free!

TODAY, the murderous invaders lie dead in the thousands, many of them still clinging greedily to their stolen gold.

Last night the Spanish leader made a foolish mistake. Having realized that he could not easily defeat us, Cortés decided to lead his army out of our city. And knowing that we Aztecs rarely fight at night, he waited until it was dark to escape. The gods seemed to be on his side. There was no moon, and the night was pitch-black.

The Spaniards and their Tlaxcalan allies crept through the city toward the lake, hoping to sneak across the eastern causeway to the mainland.

But they had barely reached the edge of the city when they were seen by some women fetchin water from the lake.

These brave wome swiftly gave the alarm and the whole city aros to give chase.

TRAPPED AT THE GAP

As the enemy fled, ou warriors took to thei canoes. They planned t trap the Spaniards an Tlaxcalans at the firs of the four gaps in th causeway and to attac them from the water.

Our warriors though the enemy wouldn't b able to cross the gaps –

STRANGE BIRD: Was it a warning of things to come?

NOT GODS, JUST MEN

Illustrated by MAXINE HAMIL

WHY DID MONTEZUMA II treat th Spaniards as if they were gods And why did he fail us in our hour o need? *The Aztec News* investigates.

IN THE YEARS before the Spaniards arrived, our gods sent many strange signs to us. Comets wer seen flashing throug the sky in the middle o

CAUSEWAY CHAOS! The enemy die in the thousands as they attempt to flee from our city.

spears, and arrows. Some of the enemy were killed outright. Others were wounded and fell into the lake.

Many of the Spaniards drowned, weighed down by their heavy armor. In a desperate bid to escape, others clambered over the bodies of their dead comrades. And in this way a number of them managed to reach the mainland.

When day dawned and the bodies were counted, it became clear that as few as a third of the Spaniards and Tlaxcalans had gotten away.

Cortés must now be weeping like a cloud in the rainy season. Surely he will never dare to return to Tenochtitlán. ◼

as usual, the wooden bridges that span them had been removed to prevent anyone from entering our city at night.

But knowing this, the Spaniards had built their own bridge. Only when they came to the second gap in the causeway did they realize their mistake. The Spaniards had only one bridge, and the last of their army was still using it to cross the first gap!

By this time our warriors had reached the causeway in their canoes. And now they let loose a deadly hail of stones,

the day. Lightning struck, destroying a temple, but no thunder was heard. And then a fisherman brought a strange bird to the royal palace.

The bird had a mirror on its head in which the stars could be seen. But when Montezuma looked into the mirror, he saw rows of armed warriors marching to war.

No one knew what to make of these omens.

And then the strangers arrived. They came from the east, and our god Quetzalcoatl was known to have sailed away in that direction hundreds of years ago.

Was the strangers' leader, Cortés, the god Quetzalcoatl returning to his people?

If this had been the case, then Montezuma was wise to treat Cortés as a god — showering

gifts on him and inviting him to stay in our city.

But before long it became clear that Cortés was a man, not a god. And when the Spaniards

FIRST IMPRESSIONS: Cortés and Montezuma II meet.

killed our nobles and stole our gold, we should have acted immediately.

Yet instead of ordering our warriors to attack, Montezuma behaved like

a coward. He did whatever Cortés told him to, even asking us to lay down our weapons and surrender.

Is it any wonder then that our nobles decided to replace Montezuma?

We pray that our new ruler, Cuitlahuac, has the strength of the jaguar and the wisdom of the eagle. May the gods help him to drive the Spaniards into the sea. ◼

TIME TO CHANGE TACTICS

FIGHTING FIT: Our Jaguar and Eagle warriors.

WE HAVE FORCED the enemy out of Tenochtitlán, but it has cost us the lives of many brave warriors. How did the Spaniards come to be such a threat to our people? And now that we have thrown them out of the city, can we succeed in driving them out of our empire?

The Aztec News put some tough questions to a top army commander.

❓ What's wrong with our warriors — why has it been so difficult to rid our city of the Spaniards?

The problem isn't with our men. It's with the foreigners — they don't fight like normal people!

❓ What do you mean?

Well, as you know, the main reason we Aztecs go to war is to capture as many people as possible for our priests to sacrifice at the Great Temple. It's our duty to the gods.

But the Spaniards don't take prisoners. They fight to kill — right there, on the battlefield. They don't obey other rules of war, either. We rarely fight at night or during the harvest season. But these foreigners don't seem to care when they fight, so how can we know what to expect of them?

❓ Even so, there were only a few hundred Spaniards, whereas we have 25,000 warriors. Shouldn't it have been easy to defeat them?

Possibly. But don't forget that the foreigners were supported by thousands of our Tlaxcalan enemies.

Besides, it's not just the number of men that counts. These foreigners use weapons we've never seen before. They have long swords made from a hard shiny metal and they carry fire-sticks they call guns. They also use

KILLING MACHINE:
The lethal Spanish cannon.

huge exploding tubes they call cannons.

❓ Aren't our weapons any good, then?

On the contrary, they are deadly! The obsidian glass we use to edge our wooden swords and the points of our spears and arrows is razor sharp.

But I must admit that the newcomers' weapons are far more dangerous than ours. Their swords don't break, as ours do. And you wouldn't believe the savage wounds made by their guns. A single shot from one of their

cannons can kill a whole group of men at a great distance.

The Spaniards have better armor than we do, too. They protect their heads and bodies with metal — our wooden weapons just bounce off it and break into pieces.

I'm afraid that our padded cotton armor is all but useless against the foreigners' weapons.

❓ So how do you think we should deal with the Spaniards?

Well, in spite of all that's happened, I firmly believe

BOYS TO MEN

Illustrated by SIMONE BONI

HAS THE TIME come to change the way we teach our boys to fight? *The Aztec News* takes a close look at our training methods.

ON THE DAY they're born, boys are given a toy bow with arrows. Then at school they're taught to use weapons and to obey orders.

THE NEXT STEP

At the age of 18, they go to their first Flower War, where they learn what fighting is all about.

Although these wars have been arranged in advance with a neighboring tribe, if a boy is captured, he still risks losing his life. After all,

like us, our neighbors always need captives to sacrifice to the gods.

At their first Flower War, the boys just watch. At their second, they fight in groups of four. Then, once his group has captured someone, each boy is allowed to fight on his own in the next Flower War.

Only after this can a boy call himself a warrior and take part in a real battle.

At every stage of their training, boys are taught that the more captives

they take, the greater the honor they earn — for themselves, for our nation, and for the gods.

And that's not all. Warriors can earn rich rewards. A man who single-handedly takes four captives becomes a noble and may join the Jaguars or the Eagles — the two finest warrior groups in our army.

Our training methods produced the men who won us a mighty empire and made our army a legend in the land. How can we possibly improve upon that?

DRESSED TO KILL: Spanish soldiers in their metal armor.

Illustrated by CHRISTIAN HOOK

that our warriors are the finest in the world, and that in time they will defeat the enemy.

Of course, we could try copying the foreigners' weapons and armor. And perhaps even their tactics, too, such as the way they fight in groups to protect one another.

But the Spaniards fight to kill, and we couldn't possibly do this. It would be an insult to our gods. Our whole religion is

centered around capturing prisoners for sacrifice. And every life taken on the battlefield would be one fewer that we could offer to our gods.

Do you think the Spaniards will return to Tenochtitlán?
Well, let's hope not. But even if they don't, we should still go after them and drive them right out of our empire.

It will be a long and bitter struggle, but with the gods on our side, we are sure to triumph in the end.

NEVER TOO YOUNG TO START: War training begins while boys are still in school.

ROYALTY REVEALED

Illustrated by SIMONE BONI

IT'S LONELY AT THE TOP: Nobles and visitors from other tribes keep a respectful distance while our great ruler takes a stroll in the palace gardens.

OUR GREAT RULER may live in the heart of our city, but only nobles are allowed into his palace. The rest of us know little about his life — until now, that is. *The Aztec News* brings you this exclusive interview with a palace official.

❓ What do you think is our ruler's most important duty?

It's hard to say. Our ruler has many responsibilities. He is the head of the priesthood, the law courts, and the army. But I'd say his most important job is representing our nation.

He speaks to the gods on our behalf, as well as to the rulers of other tribes. That's why we call him Tlatoani, the Speaker, of course.

❓ But he doesn't have to do all this single-handedly, does he?

Oh, no! The day-to-day running of Tenochtitlán is done by his deputy, the Snake Woman — along with hundreds of hard-working officials such as myself, I might add.

❓ Yet the Snake Woman is really a man. Can you explain how the title came about?

But of course. The Snake Woman is named after the goddess Cihuacoatl.

And the fact that the second-most-important man in the empire takes his name from a goddess rather than a god shows how highly we honor women in our society.

❓ Most of our readers are unfamiliar with the Tlatoani's palace. Could you describe it for us?

Certainly — but there are so many rooms, it's hard to know where to begin! As well as thousands of bedrooms, there are huge dining halls and libraries, some so vast that they take your breath away. The treasure house and law court are magnificent, too. And the beautiful gardens are a joy to visit, as is the royal zoo.

❓ How many people live in the palace?

Let's see now. The royal family itself is pretty extensive — the ruler has many beautiful wives — and they are waited on by at least 3,000 servants.

Then there are the guests — there may be as many as 600 visiting rulers and nobles here every day.

❓ And is it your job to tell visitors to the palace how to behave?

Indeed it is. I'm always having to remind nobles to wear their plainest clothes when they meet with our ruler.

They have to take off their shoes, too. Only the Tlatoani's close advisers may wear shoes in his presence. And no one is ever allowed to turn his back on him or look directly at his face.

❓ It must be amazing to be treated with so much respect.

I suppose so. But I often think that the Tlatoani's life must be very lonely. I mean, how many real friends can he have when no one is allowed to look him in the eye?

KNOW YOUR PLACE!

An increasing number of commoners has been seen wearing cotton clothes. This is a luxury allowed only to nobles. Commoners are reminded that they are forbidden to wear any clothing not woven from the fiber of the maguey cactus.

✻

OFFENDERS WILL BE TAKEN INTO SLAVERY.

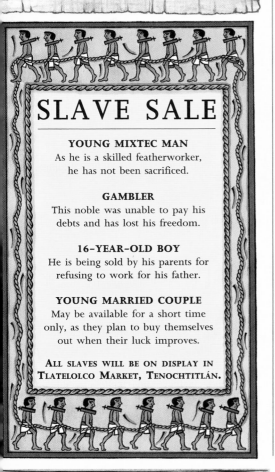

THE PRICE OF POWER

Illustrated by LUIGI GALANTE

HAVE YOU EVER wondered what life would be like as a noble? If so, remember that life at the top isn't everything it's cracked up to be.

OF COURSE, there are many benefits to being a noble. For starters, they're seriously rich! Apart from anything else, whenever tribute payments are sent to our great ruler by conquered peoples, every noble is given a share of the goods.

And, as we all know, nobles can have two-story houses and live right in the city center.

Then, there's the fact that noblemen are able to marry as many women as they want to. And they and their families

NOBLE: Fine clothes, but is it all fun and games?

are allowed to wear top-quality clothing, like long cotton or feather capes, and jewelry made from gold and precious stones.

Commoners, on the other hand, can't wear any jewelry other than clay-bead or shell necklaces and earrings. And may the gods help them if they're ever seen in anything not made out of maguey-cactus cloth!

TWO SIDES TO EVERY STORY

But there's a downside to everything, of course.

For example, if a noble is found guilty of a crime, he'll be punished far more harshly than a commoner. A commoner caught for a particular crime might be forced into slavery, but a noble might lose his life for the same offense.

Then there are your children to think of. As a noble, you'll probably send them to a calmecac school so they'll get a better choice of job when they grow up. If they study hard, they may

COMMONER: A simple life, but a happy one?

even become a judge, a general, or a priest. But as calmecac students aren't ever allowed to visit their homes, you'll never get to see them.

As a commoner, you will probably prefer your children to go to a local telpochcalli school. They may have to sleep there, but at least they'll be free to come home to eat with you every day.

The simple truth of the matter is you're better off the way you are. So count your blessings — and just be glad that you're an Aztec!

TENOCHTITLÁN, A GUIDE

Illustrated by PETER VISSCHER

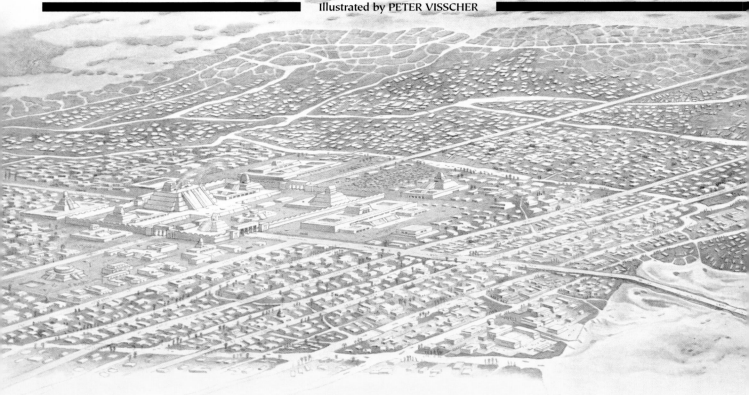

HEART OF THE CITY: The Great Temple stands at the center of Tenochtitlán — use it as a landmark and you'll never get lost.

OUR BEAUTIFUL CITY attracts visitors from all over the empire, but finding your way around can be tricky. So let *The Aztec News* help you to make the most of your stay in Tenochtitlán.

YOUR FIRST sight of our glorious island city will take your breath away — if, that is, you have any left after the long climb over the mountains that surround Lake Texcoco!

As you come down into the valley, you'll see Tenochtitlán glimmering in the distance ahead of you, like a golden jewel set in jade green water. It may not look so big from where you are now, but you'll soon discover that it's vast. Covering nearly 6 square miles, our city is home to more than 250,000 people.

GETTING AROUND

Once you reach the lake's edge, you have a choice. You can either paddle across the water in a dugout canoe, or you can enter the city by one of three long causeways, all of them wide enough for eight people to walk along side by side.

Once in Tenochtitlán, you can also choose to travel by canoe or walk, as the city is crisscrossed by a network of canals and streets.

But be warned, the canals can be very smelly. You might find yourself traveling next to a canoe taking sewage from the city's public toilets to enrich the soil of the chinampas — the farms at the edge of our island.

But don't let this stop you from taking a trip around the chinampas. Paddle out there some fine evening, then drift through the peaceful tunnels of leaves — it's a truly unforgettable experience!

SIGHTSEEING

Towering above the city skyline is our famous Great Temple with its twin shrines. One shrine is to Huitzilopochtli, the awesome god of the sun, war, and our nation. The other is to Tlaloc, our mighty god of rain.

Sadly, only nobles are allowed inside the Great Square where the temple stands. But even if you aren't permitted to enter the square, you'll be able to glimpse the shrine over the high stone wa that surrounds it.

Around the outside o the square are the thre royal palaces and th houses of the nobles.

But to discover how ordinary people live, hea out of the city center t the busy streets that li beyond. Here you'll fine whitewashed cottages noisy with turkeys, dogs and children.

EATING OUT

Our city is well know for its mouthwatering tortilla pancakes — bu

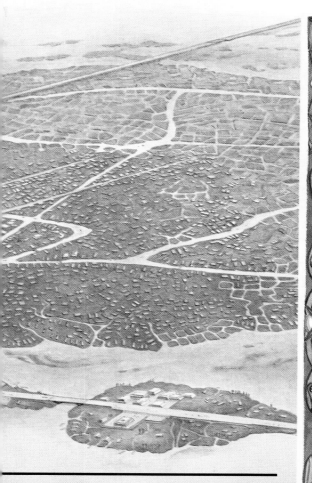

one from a street vender. Don't be tempted to try a cup of pulque, though. It's made from the juice of the maguey cactus and is alcoholic, so it's banned to all except the elderly.

But who needs alcohol when the water tastes so delicious? Fresh from mountain springs, it is carried into the city by aqueducts.

SOUVENIRS

Whatever you're looking for, from the simple to the exotic, the place to go is Tlatelolco Market. To find it, just head north from the Great Square. Most traders will accept a variety of goods in exchange for their wares, but you might find it easier to take along some cocoa beans or pieces of copper instead.

FESTIVALS

If you can, go to one of our religious festivals while you're in the city — there's at least one every month. The costumes, dancing, and music at these spectacular events will make your visit to Tenochtitlán one you'll always remember! ✵

PROUD OF YOUR CITY?

MORE AND MORE visitors come to Tenochtitlán every year. Do they see clean streets and well-tended farms? That depends on you and your calpulli.

A CALPULLI is more than just a neighborhood, it's a way of life. There are around 80 calpulli in our city now, and each one relies on every person living in it to keep things running smoothly.

But some calpulli are better than others — try our quiz to see how yours shapes up!

HOW TO SCORE

Score one point for each of the following duties carried out in the past month by your calpulli:

STREET CLEANING
a) Were the streets in your calpulli swept daily?
b) Were they sprinkled with water every day to keep down the dust?

WASTE DISPOSAL
a) Was the sewage taken to the chinampas for use as manure?
b) Was garbage carted away into the lake?

MILITARY TRAINING
a) Did the schools provide proper weapons training?
b) Were the men ready to be called up to fight?

EDUCATION
a) Was every child at school during the day?
b) Afterward, did they attend the House of Song?

RELIGIOUS DUTIES
a) Was the local temple swept out regularly?
b) Were all the streets decorated at festival time?

COMMUNITY CARE
a) Were all sick people properly looked after?
b) Were the elderly given enough food to eat?

HOW DID YOU DO?
Score: 1–4 Your calpulli is a disgrace — get down to work!
Score: 5–9 There's room for improvement — get together with your neighbors to see what can be done.
Score: 10+ Your calpulli is a credit to our city and our nation!

UNDER COVER

Illustrated by LUIGI GALANTE

OUR TRAVELING merchants, the pochtecas, are often envied for their great wealth. But the trade reporter of *The Aztec News* believes that their riches are well earned in view of the dangers they face.

I REMEMBER the very first time I saw the pochtecas. I was 5 years old. It was a hot night and I couldn't sleep, so I wandered out onto the road.

There, in the moonlight, I saw a long line of porters shuffling by, straining beneath their loads. And leading them were shadowy figures dressed in capes.

"Who are those men?" I asked my mother.

"They're pochtecas," she said, smiling. "They are the merchants who bring in marvelous things for us to buy at the market.

They carry so much wealth with them that they travel under the cover of darkness for fear of robbers. And they store their goods in secret warehouses in the city."

My mother went on to talk of the far-off lands the pochtecas visited and of the many treasures they brought back — golden jewelry, feather capes, tortoiseshell cups, spices, cocoa beans. . . .

Of course, it wasn't surprising that I hadn't yet come across these merchants. They keep to

BY THE LIGHT OF THE MOON: Three pochtecas and their porters quietly leave the city.

themselves. They live in a separate part of the city and have their own temples and laws. They even have their own god —Yacatecuhtli.

But when I was a young warrior marching across the empire with the army I often saw these merchants trading in faraway cities. And I began to realize that it's the pochtecas who help to make our city so rich. Since then, I've wondered if they do more than just buy and sell. . . .

I SPY A TRADER

I've heard people say that the pochtecas spy for our ruler in the lands they visit. We can't know this for certain, of course, but they do have the perfect cover — they speak many languages, and they do their best to blend in with other tribes.

There's no question that many pochtecas are even richer than nobles. But then, traveling beyond the borders of the empire can be dangerous — let alone spying! Personally, I admire their courage, and I have ever since that magical night when I was a little boy. ◢

MARKET FORCES

Illustrated by ANGUS MᶜBRIDE

YOU CAN HEAR the noise of the crowd from more than 3 miles away! But why is Tlatelolco Market so popular? *The Aztec News* asked a market trader . . .

WE SELL what the public wants to buy — it's as simple as that!

Whether it's quality cotton garments made by local craftworkers, fine jewelry and featherwork brought in by pochtecas, or the fresh fruit and vegetables grown by our farmers — you'll find it all here.

We get up to 60,000 people buying and selling every day. But the market wouldn't be so successful if it weren't so organized.

That's why there's a committee of merchants to make certain that the market is properly run. The committee ensures that everyone trades fairly — anyone caught dealing in poor-quality goods is severely punished. It also keeps an eye on how much traders ask for their goods. But of course not everything is cheap.

The market is split up into different areas, too, according to what's for sale, so it's easy for people to find what they want.

In the food section, for example, you can buy everything from wild duck and pigeon to tasty dog meat, goose eggs, and salted fish. While nearby, there'll be cocoa beans, vanilla pods, avocados, guavas, cherries. . . .

COME AND GET IT!

In fact, whatever you need, we've got it. You'll find sleeping mats and storage jars, firewood and flowers, brooms and baskets. You can even buy a slave or two to help around the house.

Tlatelolco is more than just a market, though. If you're feeling ill, we've got doctors who can tell you what the problem is and sell you the ointments or herbs that you need.

You can get a haircut or a shave, have your fortune read, or just meet with friends over a cup of frothy chocolate.

There's so much to buy and do at Tlatelolco Market — that's why so many people come here. And as far as we traders are concerned, the more the merrier!

SHOP TILL YOU DROP! Tlatelolco Market, where everything from turkeys to terra-cotta pots is for sale.

GIFT OF BLOOD

Illustrated by MIKE BOSTOCK

THE SPANIARDS HAVE threatened our entire way of life, not only with their weapons and way of fighting, but with their attitude toward our religion. *The Aztec News* **asked a priest at the Great Temple for his opinion.**

QUETZALCOATL
God of knowledge and creation

XIPE TOTEC
God of springtime

CHANTICO
Goddess of the hearth

THE FOREIGNERS call us cruel because we sacrifice people to our gods. But what do they know about our beliefs?

THE FIRST SACRIFICE

They don't realize how, at the very beginning of our history, the gods sacrificed themselves so that we could live. And neither do they seem to understand that if we don't repay our gods for this selfless act, the earth will be destroyed.

Is it not obvious that if we fail to honor our gods and goddesses with our blood, they'll become angry and turn their backs on us?

Huitzilopochtli must be constantly fed with blood and prayers, or he will leave us. And if

this happens, then who will protect us?

And if we stop sacrificing children to Tlaloc in the spring, their tears will no longer bring the rain to make the crops grow.

If the Spaniards can't understand how vital it is for us to give blood to the gods, how can they understand what an honor it is to be chosen as a sacrifice?

How can they say we are cruel to send someone to a carefree life after death? After

all, the reward for those chosen is the same as that given to men who die in battle and to women who die in childbirth. They become the companions of the sun. Then, after four years, they return to Earth as butterflies or hummingbirds.

DARKNESS AHEAD

Only those who have died such heroic deaths are honored in this way. When the rest of us die, we have to go to Mictlan, the place of darkness.

My message to the readers of *The Aztec News* is listen to the words of your own priests, not to those of strangers. If we look after our gods, they'll look after us.

HUITZILOPOCHTLI
God of war, the sun, and our nation

TEZCATLIPOCA
God of fate and creation

CHICOMECOATL
Goddess of maize

TLALOC
God of rain

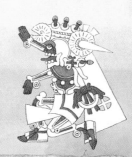

MICTLANTECUHTLI
God of the dead

CHALCHIUHTLICUE
Goddess of lakes and streams

HOLY LIFE IS VERY HARD

Illustrated by LUIGI GALANTE

IT IS A PROUD moment for all noble parents when their son becomes a priest. But do you really know what kind of life your son is getting himself into?

YOU SHOULD realize that if your son is thinking of becoming a priest, he is going to have to work very hard indeed.

He may find the hours long at calmecac school, and the teachers strict, but when he becomes a trainee priest, his life will be far more difficult!

When he is 17 years old, your son will be able to join a local temple in your calpulli. Then he will have the honor of painting his body black to show that he's a priest.

He'll have to get up before dawn every day to perform his duties — from blowing a conch-shell trumpet to make sure that everybody in the calpulli wakes up to burning incense as an offering to the gods.

STUDY BY DAY, PRAY BY NIGHT

And there'll be plenty of studying to do, too. Your son will be taught how to read the patterns of the stars so that he can try to predict the future. And he'll have to learn the many religious songs that are chanted at festivals.

He'll also be expected to pierce his body with cactus spines until his blood flows and to take special herbs to give him holy visions.

Even after dark there is little rest for priests. Your son will spend many nights in the mountains that surround our lake, praying to the gods.

But if he works hard, your son can hope to rise to a higher rank within the priesthood every few years.

And eventually he may be able to perform the most important priestly duty of all — honoring the gods with gifts of human sacrifice. 🔳

TIME TO GET UP: A priest gives the morning alarm call.

ALL WRAPPED UP

SAYING GOOD-BYE TO A LOVED ONE?

We can supply everything you need for a loved one's funeral — from cloth for wrapping the dead body to flowers, feathers, and colored paper for decorating the funeral bundle.

Also available — pottery urns for storing the ashes once the funeral bundle has been burned.

DYING TO PLEASE, TLATELOLCO MARKET, TENOCHTITLÁN

THE EATING OF MAIZE AND BEANS FESTIVAL

To celebrate the end of the dry season, the senior priest of the Great Temple respectfully requests noble lords to prepare for the dance of the maize stalks. Commoners are reminded to decorate their homes and local calpulli temples with reeds from the lake.

FEVER PITCH!

Illustrated by CHRIS MOLAN

MAY MACUILXOCHITL, the god of dice, preserve us. Our games are supposed to be played in honor of our gods, but these days they seem to be little more than an excuse for gambling.

IT IS SAID that we Aztecs will bet on anything. And it's true, gambling is in our blood. Just watch a game of patolli taking place. There's always a crowd of onlookers cheering, arguing, and of course, placing bets.

RICH MAN, POOR MAN?

And the betting stakes aren't just beans. Commoners will often gamble away all their possessions. And the nobles are no better,

particularly when they bet on the ball game tlachtli. Some have lost everything they own — their jewels and clothes, their slaves and homes, and even their land.

It might seem like a bit of harmless fun, but gambling can ruin lives. One noble was so sure of a tlachtli result that he even bet himself — he lost and ended up as a slave!

So the next time you feel tempted to place a bet, turn to the gods instead, and offer up a prayer. ✳

DON'T BET ON IT: Play patolli only to honor the gods.

RINGSIDE ACTION: Tlachtli players strive for the ultimate goal — a ring shot.

GODLY GAME

Illustrated by GINO D'ACHILLE

EVEN THE GODS play tlachtli, so it's no wonder we mortals take this sport so seriously. *The Aztec News* asked one leading player what the game means to him.

❓ Does tlachtli still have religious meaning for you?
Absolutely! The gods themselves play tlachtli, you know. They use the sky as their court and the sun as their ball. And

the priests watch every single game we play. They use the results of the matches to predict what will happen in the future — what could be holier than that?

All the players take

tlachtli very seriously, too. None of us would ever begin a game without first praying to the gods and burning incense as an offering to them.

❓ What first attracted you to tlachtli?
Oh, the excitement of the game — it's just like going into battle.

When I put on my leather arm protector,

and team colors and walk out onto the court, I know I've got hours of the toughest, fastest, most skillful game in the land ahead of me. And with the crowds waving and cheering us on, the atmosphere is fantastic. I tell you — it's the best feeling in the world.

What kind of skills do you need?
Speed, judgment, timing. That rubber ball is fast — it bounces and skitters all over the place. You've got to be quick to get control of it.

You need to be agile, too. It's a foul if you handle or kick the ball, so we have to leap and twist in the air and then bounce the ball off our hips and elbows.

Points are scored for skillful moves, as well as for possession of the ball and, of course, for a ring shot. That's the ultimate — a shot through one of the stone rings on either side of the court. It takes real skill, as the rings are set high above your head in the wall. But what a feeling when you score — it's incredible!

And the players are well rewarded?
Absolutely. If you score a ring shot, you win some great prizes — you can even take home one of the spectators' capes. Once the game has finished, people run for the exits pretty quickly, I can tell you.

You become famous, too — thousands of fans welcome you wherever you go. But I have to say that for me the real thrill comes from playing the game itself and knowing that I've brought honor not only to myself and my team, but also to the gods.

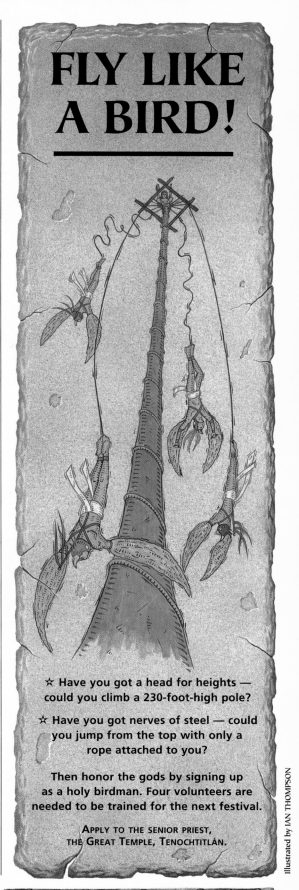

FLY LIKE A BIRD!

☆ **Have you got a head for heights — could you climb a 230-foot-high pole?**

☆ **Have you got nerves of steel — could you jump from the top with only a rope attached to you?**

Then honor the gods by signing up as a holy birdman. Four volunteers are needed to be trained for the next festival.

APPLY TO THE SENIOR PRIEST, THE GREAT TEMPLE, TENOCHTITLÁN.

Illustrated by IAN THOMPSON

YOUTH OF TODAY

Illustrated by SUE SHIELDS

PUT YOUR BACK INTO IT! Other girls look on as a student finishes her weaving on a back-strap loom.

WITH TWO KINDS of schools to choose from, it can be hard to know which one is best for your child. To help you make a decision, here's what two students have to say about their school days.

NOBLE'S SON

Because I come from a noble family, my father thought I should go to a calmecac school.

At first I hated it. I was only 6 years old, and we calmecac pupils not only sleep at school, we eat all our meals here, too, so we never get to see our parents. At least the students at telpochcalli schools eat with their family every day.

I don't get to see my sister either, even though we're at the same school. Girls are taught separately — they learn things like embroidery and weaving.

Our teachers are really strict, too. They make us boys get up in the middle of the night to pray to the gods, and they make us do boring jobs like chopping wood and sweeping

NO MORE KISSING PLEASE!

WHAT'S GOING ON at the Houses of Song? Are standards slipping? *The Aztec News* reprints a letter we received from an angry parent.

WHEN I WAS a child and went to my local House of Song every day after school, we spent all our time playing musical instruments, practicing the steps of our national dances, and studying our traditional songs.

But things seem to have changed somewhat since my day. What is the point of keeping girls and boys separated at school if they are allowed to talk freely with one another at the Houses of Song? And from what I hear, it isn't just talking either!

Several parents have admitted to me that their daughters have confessed

SPEAK OUT

floors. And if they catch us being lazy they jab us with cactus spines!

Of course now that I'm older I realize how lucky I am. In addition to weapons practice, we calmecac boys study all kinds of things — astronomy, math, and history, as well as reading and writing picture symbols. So when I leave school, I know I'll get a good job.

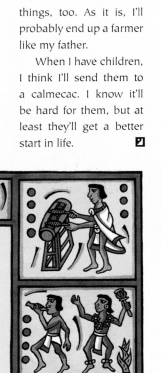

Cartoon by MARTIN BROWN

THIS'LL TEACH HIM!

COMMONER'S SON

My father sent me to a telpochcalli. He thought I'd rather be at a local school with friends from my calpulli than go to a calmecac in the city center with lots of noble children I don't know.

He was right — the telpochcalli is more fun. But we don't study as many subjects as they do at calmecacs.

When we aren't doing chores like cleaning the streets or digging canals, we telpochcalli boys seem to spend most of our time at weapons practice.

I know this training will make me a better warrior, but I'd have liked the chance to learn other things, too. As it is, I'll probably end up a farmer like my father.

When I have children, I think I'll send them to a calmecac. I know it'll be hard for them, but at least they'll get a better start in life.

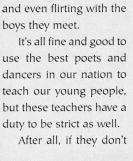

to giggling, whispering, and even flirting with the boys they meet.

It's all fine and good to use the best poets and dancers in our nation to teach our young people, but these teachers have a duty to be strict as well.

After all, if they don't

teach our children to have a proper respect for our beliefs, who will?

Houses of Song are for learning the customs and traditions of our people — not for kissing and cuddling. And the sooner our children realize this, the better!

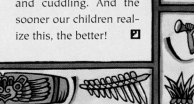

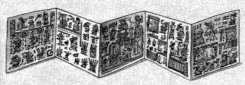

PAMPER YOUR CHINAMPA

Illustrated by PETER VISSCHER

SURROUNDED BY WATER: Our farmers not only grow crops on their chinampas, they build their homes on them, too.

MAINLAND FARMERS often ask how we Aztecs manage to grow crops on chinampas, the "floating farms" around the edges of our island. So here, specially for them, *The Aztec News* reveals some of the secrets of our farmers' success.

VISITORS TO our city are often amazed at the way our farmers manage to create new land and grow crops in the middle of a lake. It's not really that difficult, but there are a few basic rules.

RULE 1: Build a strong chinampa.

Our farmers start by pushing long wooden poles into the lakebed to mark out a new plot.

Some chinampas are only a few yards long. Others are big enough to build a house on and still have plenty of room for farmland. The size doesn't really matter, as long as there's enough room between each one for two canoes to pass each other.

Next, reed fences are lashed to the poles to enclose the plot. The plot is then filled with mud dredged up from the bottom of the lake.

Finally, lots of willow trees are planted around all four sides of the chinampa. These trees grow very quickly, and their tangled roots bind the soil and stop it from being washed away.

VERY HANDY: A digging stick is a farmer's main tool.

RULE 2: Take good care of your soil.

Lake mud makes for rich soil, but it has to be treated well. So our farmers regularly shovel in lots of vegetable compost and sewage from the city toilets. It's a smelly job, but all this care does pay off. Our farmers can grow up to seven crops a year, one after another.

RULE 3: Plant the right crops at the right time.

Without the food grown on the chinampas, we'd starve, so it's only fair that farmers are given as much help as possible. Farming experts tell them when to plant seeds and harvest crops.

The main crop is maize, but all kinds of vegetables and fruit are grown as well — from chilis, sweet potatoes, and beans to avocados, tomatoes, and guavas.

Flowers are grown too — some for selling at the market, some for religious festivals, and others, such as marigolds, because they keep insect pests away.

RULE 4: Work hard!

Each calpulli runs its own chinampas according to strict rules.

If a farmer is lazy, his land is taken away from him and given to someone who is prepared to work harder.

DEAR DOCTOR

Illustrated by MIKE BOSTOCK

THE MEDICAL TEAM at *The Aztec News* is made up of men and women who are experts in the use of herbal medicines, magic, and surgery. Over the years they have answered hundreds of your letters on all sorts of problems. Here are just a few of them. . . .

❓ I've been sick with a fever for weeks. Can you suggest anything that will help?

You should be taking regular steam baths. If you don't have a steam hut of your own, use a friend's. Not only will the steam clean and relax you, the heat will make you sweat out the evil spirits that are poisoning your body.

❓ My face is swollen. Should I put some liquid rubber in my ears?

No, that will only work if you have an earache. The remedy for you is fried chameleon. Eating this meat will make you throw up, which will get rid of the poison inside your face and so reduce the swelling.

❓ I hurt my leg and now I can't walk. Please, can you help me?

You must get a doctor to examine your leg at once. If you've broken it, the doctor will strap on a splint. However, if you've cut your leg, the doctor will sprinkle ground-up obsidian glass on the wound to help it heal.

❓ My young son has been sniveling with a rotten cold for weeks. What should I do?

Collect dew from the fields and put a drop into each of your son's nostrils twice a day. His cold will disappear in no time.

❓ I am expecting a baby. What advice can you give me?

I imagine you've already found a good midwife to deliver the baby. But you should also follow these simple rules:

1) If you have to go out after dark, carry some wood ash with you to ward off ghosts — if you see one, this could harm your unborn child.

2) Don't chew gum, or your baby's mouth will swell up.

3) Don't look at the sun during an eclipse, or your baby will be deformed.

4) Pray to one of our goddesses of women, such as Toci, every day.

❓ My father has been suffering from terrible chest pains. Is there anything he can take?

There are several herbal remedies for chest pain — maize porridge mixed with passionflower bark is particularly good.

Never make up your own herbal remedies, though, as some plants cause strange dreams. Always get advice from a qualified doctor.

water   steam   fire

GUACAMOLE: MASHED AVOCADOS, TOMATOES AND MILD CHILLI PEPPERS

THREE-BEAN STEW WITH HOT CHILLIS

STEWED SQUASH OR PUMPKIN

RED TOMATOES AND HOT CHILLI PEPPERS

FRIED WHITE FISH WITH UNRIPENED PLUMS

TAKE AWAY A TORTILLA TODAY!

ARE YOU TIRED OF EATING THE SAME OLD TORTILLA TOPPINGS DAY AFTER DAY? THEN TANTALIZE YOUR TASTEBUDS WITH OUR NEW RANGE OF SENSATIONAL SAUCES — THEY'RE REALLY TASTY!

Takeout Tortillas, Tlatelolco Market, Tenochtitlán

FRESH TADPOLES WITH SMALL RED CHILLIS

BARBECUED TURKEY WITH GREEN CHILLIS

DOG-MEAT STEW WITH SAGE LEAVES

SWEET-POTATO STEW

FRIED DUCK-EGG SPECIAL

CALLING ALL COOKS

OUR CLAY COMAL GRIDDLES ARE GUARANTEED TO COOK A PERFECT TORTILLA EVERY TIME. ALSO AVAILABLE — STONES AND ROLLERS FOR GRINDING MAIZE INTO CORNMEAL.

THE KITCHEN STALL, TLATELOLCO MARKET, TENOCHTITLÁN

IT'S FROTHY!

We take the finest ground cocoa beans and honey and whisk them together to make the best hot chocolate in town. Try some today.

SWEET TREATS, TLATELOLCO MARKET, TENOCHTITLÁN

A CHOICE CHEW

We stock chicle — chewing gum made from the milky juice of the sapodilla tree. You can't chew a better gum!

Choosy Chews, Tlatelolco Market, Tenochtitlán

BOWLED OVER!

QUALITY DRIED VEGETABLE GOURDS — CHEAPER AND LIGHTER THAN POTTERY JUGS AND POTS.

GORGEOUS GOURDS, TLATELOLCO MARKET, TENOCHTITLÁN

NO GREATER DISH

Make grating chilis a pleasure not a chore with one of our top-quality grooved grating dishes.

GRATE IDEAS, TLATELOLCO MARKET, TENOCHTITLÁN

GIRL TALK

Illustrated by CHRIS MOLAN

ARE YOU 16 and beginning to wonder how your life will change once you're married? *The Aztec News* asked a professional matchmaker what sort of advice she gives to young brides-to-be.

TIED DOWN? A young couple's clothes are knotted together as a symbol of their marriage.

THE FIRST THING most girls want to know is what their future husband is like. I always do my best to describe him favorably, of course, even though a properly brought-up girl wouldn't dream of refusing the husband chosen for her by her family.

Mind you, some girls take a little longer than others to get used to their parents' decision! But I've yet to come across any young woman who didn't get excited about her wedding day.

After all, what girl can resist getting dressed in her best clothes, wearing traditional yellow make-up, and being the center of everyone's attention?

Marriage isn't all fun and games, though. It's a serious business, and I always make sure my girls know what their duties as wives will be.

Obviously, there's the cooking, cleaning, and weaving to do — but a wife's main responsibility is to have children.

We Aztecs love babies. "Precious feathers" we call them. Still, it's up to each mother to make sure that her children become helpful members of the family and of our nation.

CRUEL TO BE KIND

Lazy boys and girls must be punished. It's better to shut them out of the house for a night or to make their eyes sting by holding them over a fire of burning chilis, than to have naughty children.

Don't dwell on their faults, though. Children grow up quickly. Before you know it, *you'll* be visiting a matchmaker to arrange your own daughter's wedding!

HARD-TIMES HINTS

EVEN THOUGH OUR RULER keeps stores of grain to feed us when the harvest fails, we have all known times of hunger. So here are some suggestions to help you through the bad years.

◎ There are lots of edible plants growing by our lake — jicama roots are very tasty stewed, and sage leaves make good porridge. Or try some dried lake-scum cakes — after all, our warriors eat them!

◎ Our ancestors lived off snakes when they first came to our island home, so there's no reason why you can't. But if you don't fancy

snake, try opossum or frog. Tadpoles are even more delicious — add a handful to a pot of vegetable stew to give it more flavor.

◎ If things get really bad, you could always consider selling your children into slavery. It's a hard decision to have to make, but at least you know they'll be well fed by their owner.

THROWING THE

Illustrated by ANGUS MᶜBRIDE

WHETHER YOU'RE celebrating a birthday or doing your best to impress your friends, organizing a party can be hard work — unless, that is, you do it *The Aztec News* way.

THE GUEST LIST

Choose your guests with care. Nobles: You will want to invite men in positions of power who can help you or your family. Commoners: Ask as many people as you can afford, to show how generous you are.

THE PLACE TO PARTY

Make sure the seating areas for men and women are clearly separated. If you don't have enough space inside your house, a courtyard will work just as well. Decorate the area with fresh flowers, incense burners, and torches for when it gets dark.

THE MENU

Bear in mind that if your guests don't like the food you give them, they can invite themselves back again the following day for another party. So really make an effort with the menu!

If you can afford it, serve specialties like hot turkey potpies with chili and tomato sauce, or lobster with avocado. And it wouldn't be much of a party without plenty of frothy hot chocolate, would it?

Provide some pulque, too, made from the best maguey-cactus juice. But obey the law and only offer it to the elderly. You may be held responsible if anyone else gets drunk.

LET'S PARTY! Noble men and women gather for a feast.

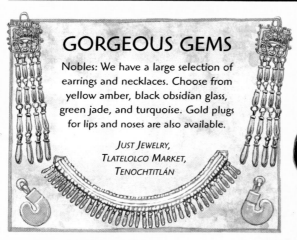

GORGEOUS GEMS

Nobles: We have a large selection of earrings and necklaces. Choose from yellow amber, black obsidian glass, green jade, and turquoise. Gold plugs for lips and noses are also available.

JUST JEWELRY,
TLATELOLCO MARKET,
TENOCHTITLÁN

HAIR TODAY

Ladies: We can supply the very best in hair products — from indigo for dyeing your hair a beautiful glossy black to colored threads and ornaments for decorating your finished style.

Tlatelolco Market, Tenochtitlán

PERFECT PARTY

ENTERTAINMENT

It goes without saying that no party is complete without music and dancing. So, if you can afford to, hire some entertainers. Otherwise, invite along a few friends who are good singers or dancers.

And there's bound to be someone who wants to play a game of patolli. But limit the gambling — your friends won't be all that happy if they end up losing a fortune!

DRESS TO IMPRESS

Everything is ready, and your guests will soon be arriving. But have you thought about what to wear? It's vital that you look your best in honor of the occasion.

Men: You'll want to wear your most brilliantly patterned cape and loin-cloth. If you're a noble, take the chance to show off your finest headdress and armbands, and your best nose- and lip-plugs.

And ladies: Make sure that your most colorful skirt and overblouse are fresh and clean.

If you're a commoner, it's worth thinking about making a new outfit — maguey cloth does look best when it's new.

Noble women should add some amber or jade earrings and perhaps a gold necklace. Precious metals and stones are forbidden to commoners, of course. Instead, wear your finest clay-bead or shell necklace.

AND FINALLY...

Don't forget that as the host of the party you will be expected to give each one of your guests a suitable present at the end of the evening.

TOWNHOUSE AVAILABLE

ONE-STORY MUD-BRICK HOUSE PERFECT FOR A COMMONER AND FAMILY, CONSISTING OF ONE BEDROOM AND A GOOD-SIZED KITCHEN WITH COOKING HEARTH.

THE HOUSE IS IN A ROW OF SIMILAR PROPERTIES, ALL FACING A BUSY STREET. BUT WITH NO ENTRANCE OR WINDOWS AT THE FRONT, YOUR PRIVACY IS GUARANTEED.

THE ENTRANCE IS AT THE REAR OF THE HOUSE, THROUGH THE ATTRACTIVE SHARED COURTYARD SHOWN ABOVE. THIS AREA IS ALSO IDEAL FOR EATING, SLEEPING, AND ENTERTAINING.

THE PROPERTY WOULD BE PARTICULARLY SUITABLE FOR A FAMILY WITH YOUNG CHILDREN, AS IT IS VERY CLOSE TO THE LOCAL TELPOCHCALLI SCHOOL.

BOX NO. 2006

FANTASTIC OFFER!

Noble's two-story stone townhouse built around a large central courtyard.

Decorated throughout with superb wall paintings, the property consists of two spacious reception rooms — one for men and one for women — as well as a dining room, kitchen, three bedrooms, steam hut, and servants' quarters.

Conveniently located in the city center, just a 5-minute walk from the Great Square.

Box No. 9531

FARMER'S COTTAGE AND CHINAMPA

As punishment for his laziness, the previous farmer has had to leave this chinampa. It is now available for a new tenant. The living quarters consists of a two-roomed thatched cottage built from mud bricks, wood, and reeds and whitewashed inside and out.

Adjoining the property is a pen for keeping turkeys or dogs, and a small steam hut. The house is in good condition, but the farmland has been badly neglected.

ONLY HARD-WORKING FARMERS NEED APPLY — BOX NO. 8354

STOP THE PRESS

JULY 1, 1521

This special edition of *The Aztec News* was intended to celebrate our magnificent empire. But in recent months it has become clear that instead it will be a final tribute to our glorious past.

Unbelievable as it seems, our gods have deserted us and we are facing ruin. Although we continue to fight to protect our city and our nation, it is likely that both will soon be destroyed.

We rejoiced when the Spaniards fled from Tenochtitlán just 13 months ago. But our joy soon turned to tears.

First, a terrifying sickness spread through our city. The Spaniards call this disease smallpox, and it stalks us like an invisible beast, killing everyone it touches. Thousands have died.

Then, at the end of December, more Spaniards arrived. Cortés now led an army of more than 900 Spanish soldiers and several thousand Tlaxcalan warriors.

By April 28, Cortés had reached Lake Texcoco. Since then, we have fought to keep him and his men out of our city. Every day our new ruler, Cuauhtémoc, leads our warriors into battle, and every evening fewer of them return. Soon we will no longer be able to keep the enemy from our causeways. Once they enter Tenochtitlán, our great nation will be no more.

May the gods have pity on us.

❀ **About A.D. 1100**
The Aztecs leave their homeland in the north of Mexico to travel south in search of a new home.

❀ **About 1195**
The Aztecs arrive in the Valley of Mexico.

❀ **1325**
The city of Tenochtitlán is founded on an island in Lake Texcoco.

The first Great Temple is built by the Aztecs in thanks to their gods.

The Aztecs have to pay tribute to the ruler of Atzcapotzalco, the most powerful city on the lake.

❀ **1375**
Acamapichtli, the first-known ruler of the Aztecs, comes to the throne.

❀ **1428**
The Aztecs join forces with the nearby cities of Texcoco and Tlacopan, forming what is known as the Triple Alliance.

Together they conquer the city of Atzcapotzalco and dominate the Valley of Mexico.

❀ **1440**
Montezuma I comes to the throne. Under his leadership the Aztec empire expands.

❀ **1486**
Ahuizotl becomes ruler. During his reign the empire continues to grow.

❀ **1502**
Montezuma II becomes ruler. The Aztec empire is now at its height.

❀ **1519**
A fleet of Spanish ships lands on the east coast of Mexico. The Spaniards set up camp at Veracruz.

Led by Hernán Cortés, the Spanish army heads toward Tenochtitlán. It is joined by warriors of the Tlaxcalan people.

Montezuma invites the Spaniards and their allies to stay in one of the royal palaces in Tenochtitlán. Once there, they take Montezuma prisoner.

❀ **1520**
Cuitlahuac, Montezuma's brother, is elected ruler. Montezuma dies, and the Spaniards flee the city.

Smallpox breaks out. Thousands die, including Cuitlahuac. Cuauhtémoc becomes the new ruler.

❀ **1521**
The Spaniards and their Tlaxcalan allies return and surround Tenochtitlán. On August 13, after a siege lasting 93 days, the Aztecs surrender and their city is destroyed. More than 240,000 Aztecs die during the siege.

❀ **1522**
Tenochtitlán is rebuilt and named Mexico City. It is declared the capital of the Spanish colony of New Spain.

AZTEC RULERS

Acamapichtli	1375–1395
Huitzilihuitl	1396–1417
Chimalpopoca	1417–1426
Itzcoatl	1427–1440
Montezuma I	1440–1469
Axayacatl	1469–1481
Tizoc	1481–1486
Ahuizotl	1486–1502
Montezuma II	1502–1520
Cuitlahuac	1520
Cuauhtémoc	1520–1521

Author: Philip Steele
Consultants:
 Penny Bateman,
 Museum Education
 Officer
 Norma Rosso,
 Museum Education
 Officer
Editor: Sarah Hudson
Designer: Louise Jackson

Ad illustrations by:
Katherine Baxter: 30t
Nicky Cooney: 19br, 30bl
Maxine Hamil: 13bl, 16bl,
 23tr, 26br, 29bm
Michaela Stewart: 23br,
 25bl & br, 26bl & bm,
 30br
George Thompson: 28bm
Mike White: 19bl, 28br

**Decorative borders and
small illustrations by:**
Simone Boni: 24bm
Vanessa Card: 3, 16br
Nicky Cooney: 15
Maxine Hamil: 1, 7, 8—9,
 10mr, 14–15, 22—23
Emily Hare: 26, 28—29
Michaela Stewart: 27
George Thompson: 10bm

With thanks to:
Linden Artists Ltd.,
Temple Rogers,
Virgil Pomfret Agency

Text copyright © 1997
by Philip Steele

Illustrations copyright
© 1997 by
Walker Books Ltd.

All rights reserved.

First U.S. paperback
edition 2000

Library of Congress
Cataloging-in-Publication
Data is available.

Library of Congress Catalog
Card Number 96-31655

ISBN 0-7636-0115-2
(hardcover)
ISBN 0-7636-0427-5
(paperback)

2 4 6 8 10 9 7 5 3

Printed in Hong Kong

This book was typeset
in Tiepolo.

Candlewick Press
2067 Massachusetts Avenue
Cambridge, Massachusetts
02140

visit us at
www.candlewick.com

PRONUNCIATION GUIDE

Ahuizotl	ah-wi-zotl
calpulli	kal-pu-lee
chinampa	chee-nam-pa
Huitzilopochtli	hwee-tsee-lo-posh-tlee
Mixtec	meesh-tek
Montezuma	mon-tay-zu-ma
patolli	pa-tol-lee
pochteca	potch-tay-kah
pulque	pul-kay
Tenochtitlán	teh-nosh-teet-lan
Texcoco	tesh-ko-ko
tlachtli	tlak-tlee
Tlaloc	tla-lok
Tlatelolco	tla-tay-lo-ko
tortilla	tor-tee-ya

❖

Some of the names used in this book
are modern ones, such as America or Mexico.
The Aztecs would have used different names.